SEARCH and RESCUE

Isabel Thomas

Chicago, Illinois

© 2008 Raintree
Published by Raintree,
an imprint of Capstone Global LLC
Chicago, Illinois

Customer Service 888–454–2279

Visit our website at www.heinemannraintree.com

Designed by Philippa Jenkins and Q2A Creative

Printed in the United States of America
in Stevens Point, Wisconsin.

062011
006273

**Library of Congress Cataloging-in-Publication
Data**
Thomas, Isabel.
    Search and rescue / Isabel Thomas.
        p. cm.
    Includes bibliographical references and index.
    ISBN-13: 978-1-4109-2850-4 (library binding)
    ISBN-10: 1-4109-2850-0 (library binding)
    ISBN-13: 978-1-4109-2867-2 (pbk.)
    ISBN-10: 1-4109-2867-5 (pbk.)
    1. Force and energy--Juvenile literature.
    2. Energy transfer--Juvenile literature.
    3. Dynamics--Juvenile literature.
    I. Title.
        QC73.4.T46 2007
        531'.6--dc22
                        2007003091

Acknowledgments
The publishers would like to thank the following
for permission to reproduce photographs: Alamy
Images pp. **12–13** (Janusz Wrobel); Corbis pp.
26–27 (Leif Skoogfors); Corbis/ GT Images pp. **6–7**
(George Tiedemann); Corbis/ Reuters pp. **18–19**;
Corbis Sygma pp. **4–5**, **8–9** (Bernard Bisson), **20–21**
(Bernard Bisson); Getty Images/ AFP pp. **14–15**; Getty
Images/ Photonica pp. **10–11**; Photolibrary/ Animals
Animals/ Earth Scenes p. **22**; Photolibrary/ Greatshots
Ltd pp. **16–17**; Science Photo Library (Dr. Arthur
Tucker) pp. **23**, **24–25** (Maximilian Stock Ltd.).

Cover photograph of a soldier looking through
binoculars reproduced with permission of Getty
Images/ AFP.

Illustrations by Mark Preston pp. 9, 12, 16, 18, 21;
    Peter Geissler pp. 28, 29

The publishers would like to thank Nancy Harris and
Harold Pratt for their assistance with the preparation
of this book.

Contents

Some words are printed in bold, **like this**. You can find out what they mean on page 30. You can also look in the box at the bottom of the page where they first appear.

"Mayday, Mayday!"

A soldier is lost in the jungle. He radios for help: "Mayday, Mayday!" Then, the radio goes dead. A team gets ready to look for him. They are **commandos**. Commandos are specially trained soldiers. They go on search-and-rescue missions. A commando never leaves another soldier in danger.

The trees in the jungle grow very close together. It is difficult to see through the trees from the air. The commandos have to go in on foot. They carry everything they need on their backs.

The commandos will use **energy** on their mission. Energy makes things happen. It can make objects move. It can make objects change shape. There are many different types of energy. Energy lets the commandos see. Energy powers their tools. Energy keeps them warm.

Every minute is important. The mission is about to begin.

commando soldier trained to go on dangerous missions
energy ability to make something happen

Commandos must be strong and fit. Their backpacks can weigh more than 50 pounds (22 kilograms). This is as heavy as a child.

5

Jungle drop

The **commandos** fly to the jungle in a helicopter. Everything that moves has **energy**. The flying helicopter has energy. It has movement energy. Movement energy is called **kinetic energy**. Big, fast objects have a lot of kinetic energy.

Energy can be changed from one type to another. The helicopter flies up. It has kinetic energy. The commandos sitting in the helicopter have **potential energy**. Potential energy is stored energy. The commandos have energy that is waiting to be used.

The commandos parachute down to the ground. As they fall, their potential energy changes. It changes back to kinetic energy. This is because they are moving. The flowchart on page 7 shows how energy changes.

The falling soldier is moving. He has kinetic energy.

kinetic energy   energy that an object has because it is moving
potential energy   energy that an object has because of where it is

The helicopter rises. It has **kinetic** (movement) energy.

The commandos are sitting in the helicopter. They have **potential** (stored) energy.

The falling commandos have **kinetic** (movement) energy.

7

The Heat Is On

The air feels hot and damp. The **commandos** look for tracks on the ground. They move through the trees. They have **kinetic** (movement) **energy**.

Everything is made of tiny pieces. These tiny pieces are called **particles**. The particles **vibrate**. This means they move back and forth all the time. The particles have a different type of kinetic energy. It is called **thermal energy**.

We cannot see thermal energy. But we can feel it. Thermal energy causes heat. The commandos feel the thermal energy (heat) of the hot air.

Hot or cold?

Hot things have fast-moving particles. The commandos boil some water. The water particles move more quickly. The water gets hotter.

gas particles (air)

particle tiny piece
thermal energy type of kinetic energy that causes heat
vibrate move back and forth quickly

Everything is made of tiny particles. The particles have kinetic (movement) energy.

solid particles (plastic)

liquid particles (water)

9

One way only

Thermal energy (heat) always flows from hot objects to cooler objects. It never flows the other way. Heat cannot travel from a cool pan to a hot fire.

Heat energy from the campfire makes the soldiers warmer.

heat transfer movement of thermal energy from one place or object to another

Setting up camp

Daylight is fading fast. The **commandos** find a clearing to camp in. They put up hammocks to sleep in. They collect wood. They build a campfire to boil water and cook food.

The campfire has a lot of **thermal energy** (heat). We cannot see thermal energy. But we notice when it moves from one place to another. This is called **heat transfer**. Heat moves from hot substances to cooler substances. The cooler substances get warmer.

Thermal energy moves from the campfire to other places. Thermal energy is transferred to the pans. It is transferred to the air. It is transferred to the soldiers. It makes them warmer.

The campfire has thermal energy (heat). → Thermal energy heats the pans.

The campfire has thermal energy (heat). → Thermal energy heats the soldiers.

Pass It On

The **commandos** cook food in a pan. Heat is transferred (moved) from the hot fire to the pan. Heat can move in three ways. The first is called **conduction**. Heat moves through a pan by conduction.

A pan is made of metal **particles** (tiny pieces). The particles **vibrate**. They move back and forth all the time. The campfire heats the bottom of the pan. The particles at the bottom of the pan begin to vibrate more quickly. They now have **thermal energy** (heat).

The fast-moving particles bump into slower particles. Some of their **energy** passes to the slow-moving particles. The slower particles begin to move more quickly, too. They now have more thermal energy. They pass it on to particles next to them.

Heat is conducted all the way through the pan. The inside gets as hot as the outside. The heat cooks the food.

conduction   way heat is transferred when particles bump into each other

cold particles

hot particles

In conduction, fast-moving particles bump into slow-moving particles. Thermal energy (heat) flows from hot parts of the pan to cooler parts of the pan.

Too hot to handle

The **commandos** are careful not to touch the hot metal pan. Metals are good **conductors**. They pass on heat when **particles** (tiny pieces) bump into each other. This is called **conduction**.

Metal particles are packed closely together. They bump into each other often. Heat is conducted (moves) quickly through a metal. Metal is a solid. Solids are the best conductors.

Many things do not conduct heat well. They are called **insulators**. Gases are good insulators. Air is a gas. Air is a good insulator. Some solids are good insulators, too. Plastic is a solid. The commandos use pans with plastic handles. Plastic is a good insulator. It does not conduct heat very well. It stays cool enough to touch.

Good insulators

Heat is lost through a person's hands and feet. Commandos wear boots with thick rubber soles. Rubber does not conduct heat well. Rubber is a good insulator. It does not take heat away from the feet.

conductor something that conducts heat well
insulator something that does not conduct heat well

Metal binoculars get very hot in the Sun. Commandos use binoculars with plastic handles. Plastic is a good insulator. It does not conduct heat very well. The plastic handles stop the commandos' hands from getting too hot.

Heat flow

The jungle gets cooler at night. The **commandos** on night watch need to stay warm. They collect water to make hot drinks. They boil it over the campfire.

Water is a liquid. It does not conduct heat as well as the metal pan. But in a few minutes all the water in the pan is hot. Heat **energy** has transferred (moved) through the water. This is called **convection**.

The metal pan is hot. It heats the water at the bottom of the pan. The hot water rises to the top. It carries **thermal energy** (heat) to the water in the rest of the pan. Cold water sinks. It fills the space left by the rising hot water. The cold water is heated up. It rises to the top of the pan. Water keeps moving around the pan. It keeps moving until all the water has the same **temperature**. This is the measure of how hot or cold something is.

Convection is the second type of **heat transfer**.

The water in the pan is heated by convection.

convection   type of heat transfer
temperature   measure of how hot or cold something is

1 Water is heated at the bottom of the pan.

2 Warm water rises.

3 Warm water carries thermal energy (heat) to the rest of the water in the pan.

4 Cold water sinks to take the place of the rising warm water.

17

Bedding down

The type of heat transfer called **convection** only happens in **fluids**. Liquids are fluids. Water is a fluid. So are gases such as air. The **particles** (tiny pieces) of a fluid can move past each other. This means that a current of heat can flow. The particles in a solid are packed close together. They cannot move past each other. A current cannot flow in a solid.

The **commandos** use sleeping bags at night. Sleeping bags stop heat from moving away from the body. A sleeping bag is full of stuffing. The stuffing contains millions of tiny air spaces. Air is a gas. The particles in air are far apart. They do not bump into each other much. They do not pass on heat by **conduction**.

The air in a sleeping bag is trapped. It cannot flow. This stops convection (hot air rising and cold air falling) from happening. The heat cannot flow in a sleeping bag. Sleeping bags are good **insulators**. They keep the commandos warm at night.

Air is trapped between the layers of a sleeping bag. Heat cannot flow by convection. The particles in air are far apart. Heat cannot travel by conduction. A sleeping bag is a good insulator.

fluid substance that flows

layers of sleeping bag

hollow fibers in sleeping bag stuffing

19

On the Trail

The next morning the **commandos** find a clue. They find a thermos in a bush. The soup inside is still warm. The missing soldier must have been there.

A thermos flask has two glass walls. The air in between the two walls is pumped out. This makes a **vacuum**. A vacuum is a totally empty space. The air has been removed.

There is one way that heat can move through a vacuum. It can move as **radiation**. Radiation is the third type of heat transfer. Radiation is **energy** that travels as waves or rays. Energy makes things happen. Energy can keep things warm. The Sun has waves or rays. This is how **thermal energy** (heat) from the Sun travels through space to Earth.

insulating lid

glass wall

soup

vacuum (totally empty space with air removed)

radiation energy that travels as waves or rays
vacuum completely empty space

The soldiers find a thermos. The soup inside is still warm. A vacuum keeps liquids hot for a long time. But it cannot keep them hot forever.

Seeing red

The **commandos** hack through the jungle. They spot fresh tracks. They think they are close to the missing soldier. But in the dark forest, it is difficult to see anything.

The team uses a **thermal camera** to look around. A thermal camera detects (sees) heat. All cameras work by recording **radiation**. Radiation is **energy** that travels as waves.

All warm objects give out a special type of radiation. Humans cannot see this type of radiation. A thermal camera records where it is coming from. The camera turns the thermal information into a picture that we can see.

A thermal camera will help the commandos spot warm objects through the thick jungle.

22

thermal camera camera that records heat radiation

This is a thermal picture. The large bird gives off radiation. A thermal camera lets us see this radiation, even when it's dark.

Key

30°C —
25°C —
20°C —
15°C —

— 90°F
— 80°F
— 70°F
— 60°F
— 55°F

The commandos look closely at the thermal pictures. They examine each warm object carefully. Hopefully, they will find the missing soldier.

Found!

The **commandos** get lucky. The **thermal camera** detects a warm patch. It is on the other side of a river. They cross the river. They watch out for crocodiles and other animals. On the other side they find signs of a campfire. The ground is still warm. There are human tracks nearby.

The tracks lead the commandos to the missing soldier! The soldier is well. But he is worried. He thinks there may be danger nearby. There is no time to lose. The commandos radio back to base for a rescue boat.

The radio is powered by **solar panels**. These panels take in light **energy** from the Sun. They change the light energy into electricity. Electricity is another type of energy. It powers the radio.

Each of these circles is a solar panel. Sunlight hits each panel. It is changed from light energy into electrical energy. The electricity is collected by wires that run over the top of each panel.

solar panel flat object that changes light energy into electrical energy

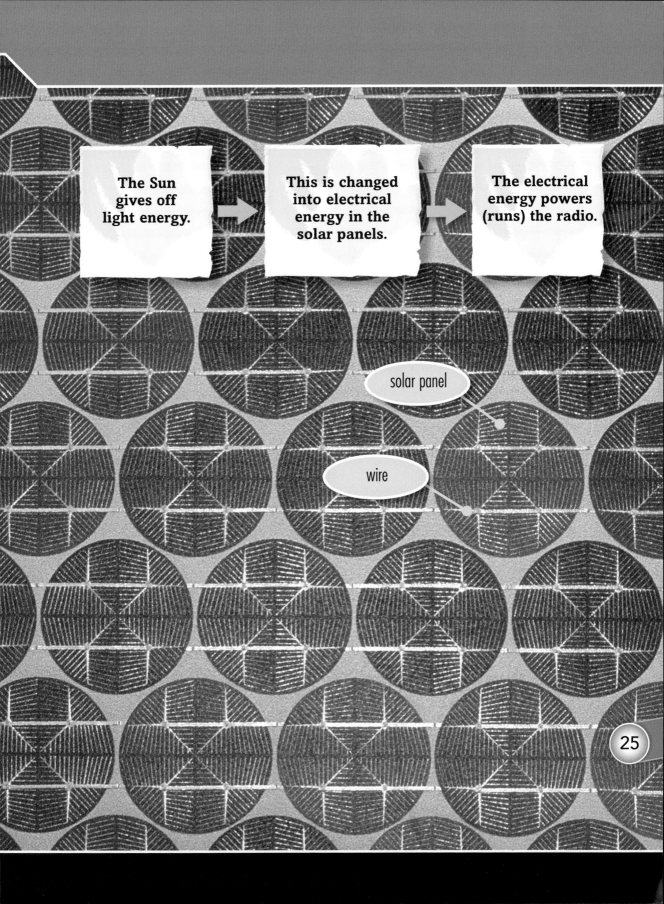

The Sun gives off light energy.

This is changed into electrical energy in the solar panels.

The electrical energy powers (runs) the radio.

solar panel

wire

26

conservation of energy scientific law that says the amount of
energy in the world stays the same

Escape from the jungle

The **commandos** hide on the riverbank. They wait for the boat to arrive. They are disguised with branches and jungle paint.

Finally, the boat arrives. The commandos climb on board. The engines roar into action. Engines burn fuel. Fuel is stored **potential energy**. Something has potential energy when it is not moving. Engines change this potential energy into **kinetic energy** (movement).

The total amount of **energy** stays the same. This is the law of **conservation of energy**. It says that energy cannot be created or destroyed. It can only be changed from one type of energy to another type of energy.

Engines change energy from fuel into kinetic, heat, and sound energy.

Mission Debrief

Back at headquarters, the **commandos** talk through the mission. **Thermal energy** (heat) helped them at every stage. **Heat transfer** carries **energy** from one place to another. This map shows the three ways that heat can be transferred. Study it carefully. It could come in handy on a mission of your own.

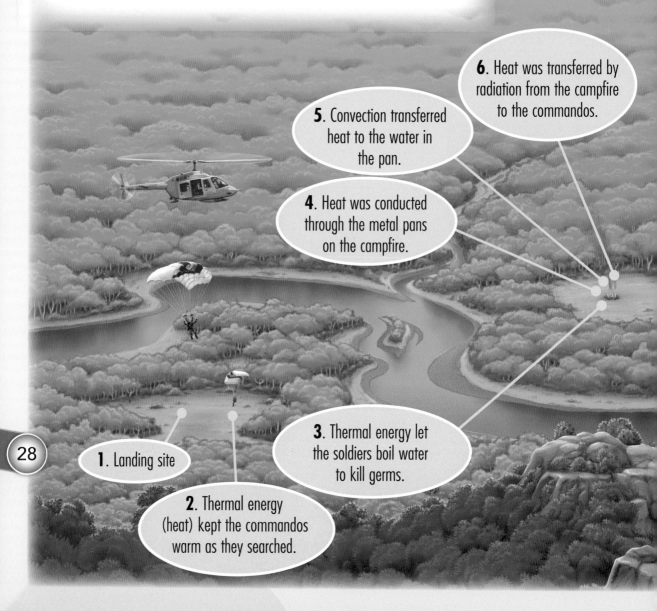

6. Heat was transferred by radiation from the campfire to the commandos.

5. Convection transferred heat to the water in the pan.

4. Heat was conducted through the metal pans on the campfire.

3. Thermal energy let the soldiers boil water to kill germs.

1. Landing site

2. Thermal energy (heat) kept the commandos warm as they searched.

Conduction
The way heat moves through a solid. The **particles** bump into each other.

Convection
The way heat flows through a liquid or a gas.

Radiation
Energy that travels as rays or waves. The Sun's heat travels to Earth as radiation.

This map of the jungle route the commandos took shows how energy can be transferred from one place to another.

10. Rescue boat

9. Solar-powered radio was used.

7. Radiation allowed the commandos to spot the missing soldier with a **thermal camera**.

8. Radiated heat from the Sun warmed the soldiers.

29

Glossary

commando soldier trained to go on dangerous missions

conduction way heat is transferred when particles bump into each other

conductor something that conducts heat well. Most metals are good conductors.

conservation of energy scientific law that says the amount of energy in the world stays the same. However, it can change from one form to another.

convection type of heat transfer. Thermal energy flows through a liquid or a gas.

energy ability to make something happen. Energy can make things move or change shape.

fluid substance that flows. Liquids and gases are fluids.

heat transfer movement of thermal energy from one place or object to another. Conduction is a type of heat transfer.

insulator something that does not conduct heat well. Rubber is a good insulator.

kinetic energy energy that an object has because it is moving

particle tiny piece. Particles are the building blocks of every solid, liquid, and gas.

potential energy energy that an object has because of where it is. A commando in a helicopter has potential energy.

radiation energy that travels as rays or waves. Light rays and microwaves are types of radiation.

solar panel flat object that changes light energy into electrical energy. A radio can be powered by solar panels.

temperature measure of how hot or cold something is

thermal camera camera that records heat radiation. We cannot see heat radiation without a thermal camera.

thermal energy type of kinetic energy that causes heat. It always flows from hot objects to cool objects.

vacuum completely empty space. Radiation can happen in a vacuum.

vibrate move back and forth quickly

Want to Know More?

Books to read

- Ball, Jackie. *Heat*. Milwaukee, W1: Gareth Stevens, 2004.

- Fullick, Ann. *Turn Up the Heat: Energy*. Chicago: Heinemann Library, 2005.

- Royston, Angela. *Conductors and Insulators*. Chicago: Heinemann Library, 2003.

Websites

- www.eia.doe.gov/kids/
  This energy website has fun facts, games, activities, and more.
- www.bbc.co.uk/science/hottopics/cooking/chemistry.shtml
  This webpage has a great animation showing how conduction, convection, and radiation can all be used to cook food.
- http://coolcosmos.ipac.caltech.edu/image_galleries/ir_zoo
  Visit the infrared zoo to see what animals look like through a thermal camera!

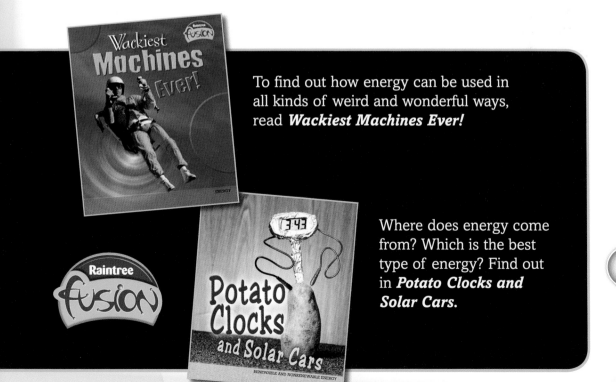

To find out how energy can be used in all kinds of weird and wonderful ways, read *Wackiest Machines Ever!*

Where does energy come from? Which is the best type of energy? Find out in *Potato Clocks and Solar Cars.*

Index

Raintree fusion

SEARCH and RESCUE

Q: A SOLDIER IS MISSING. CAN THE COMMANDOS USE ENERGY TO FIND HIM IN TIME?

Fusion delivers curriculum concepts with a high-interest twist.

➤ *Key science concepts clearly explained*

➤ *Expertly-leveled text ensures accessibility*

➤ *Vocabulary defined at point of use*

This book covers:

➤ *Thermal energy*

➤ *Conduction, convection, and radiation*

➤ *Conservation of energy*

Author

Isabel Thomas once got lost in the Amazon jungle. It was a scary experience! As a science writer, she knew how to keep warm (and scare off giant bugs) until a rescue boat arrived.

Subject Consultant

Harold Pratt is a science consultant with over 40 years of experience in the field of education.

For other fantastic **Fusion** titles, check out:
heinemannraintree.com

Heinemann
Raintree

Physical
Science
L

ISBN 978-1-4109-2867-2

9 781410 928672

S0-CNJ-301

HEAT AND ENERGY TRANSFER

NORSE MYTHOLOGY

FOR KIDS

Illustrated Myths of Gods
Goddesses, Giants
Dwarves, Elves
and other Fantastic Beings
of the Viking Saga

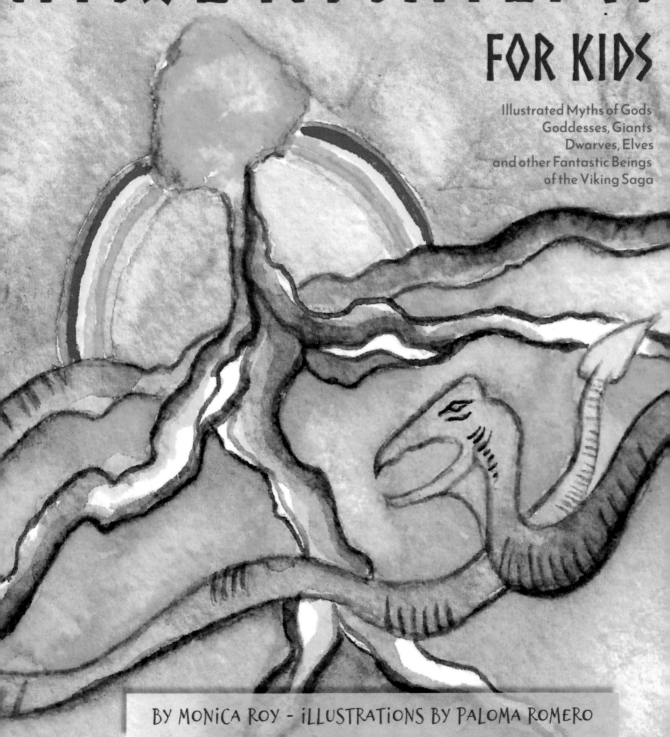

BY MONICA ROY - ILLUSTRATIONS BY PALOMA ROMERO